I CAN DRAW

COMICS
AND CARTOONS

BY FRANK C. SMITH

Wanderer Books
Published by Simon & Schuster, Inc., New York

Published by WANDERER BOOKS
A Division of Simon & Schuster, Inc.
Simon & Schuster Building
1230 Avenue of the Americas
New York, New York 10020

Manufactured in the United States of America
10 9 8 7 6 5 4 3 2

WANDERER and colophon are registered trademarks
of Simon & Schuster, Inc.

Library of Congress Cataloging in Publication Data

Smith, Frank Charles,
    I can draw comics and cartoons.

    (I can draw)
    Summary: Presents the basic techniques used in
drawing cartoon people and animals and in creating
a comic strip.
    1. Comic books, strips, etc.—Illustrations—
Juvenile literature.   2. Drawing—Technique—
Juvenile literature.   3. Cartooning—Technique—
Juvenile literature.   [1. Cartoons and comics.
2. Cartooning—Technique.   3. Drawing—Technique]
I. Title.   II. Series.
NC1764.S6   741.5   81-21989
ISBN 0-671-44490-5   AACR2

THE STICK FIGURE

TO BE ABLE TO DRAW CARTOONS WELL, START
WITH A FOUNDATION—"THE STICK FIGURE."

THINK OF THE STICK FIGURE AS A SKELETON ON WHICH A BODY CAN BE BUILT.

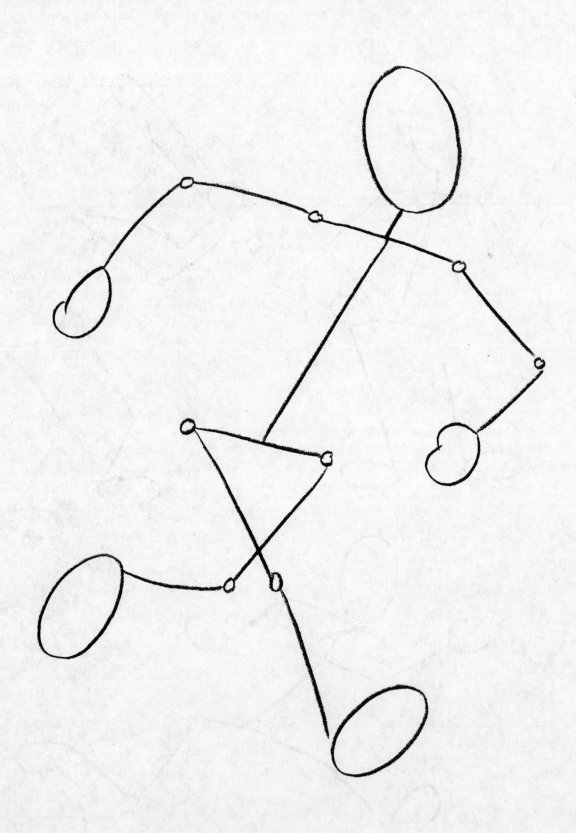

BUILD THE CARTOON CHARACTER OVER, OR ON TOP OF, THE STICK FIGURE.

THINK ABOUT HOW TO DRESS THE CHARACTER,
AND START TO PUT IN THE DETAILS.

1. THE STICK FIGURE

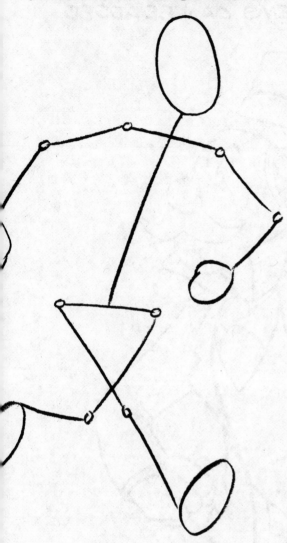

2. SHAPES FOR HEAD AND BODY

3. CONSTRUCTION

4. ADDING DETAILS

THE FINAL STEP IS THE "CLEAN UP" OF THE CHARACTER.
AT THIS POINT, ANY ADDITIONAL ITEMS CAN BE ADDED,
SUCH AS A HAT OR CANE.

CIRCLES & OVALS

AFTER THE STICK FIGURE IS DRAWN, CONSTRUCT THE CHARACTER WITH CIRCLES, EGG SHAPES, OR OVALS.

HEAD (OVAL)

ARMS AND LEGS ARE SIMPLE TOVEPIPES.

BODY COULD BE AN EGG SHAPE.

REMEMBER, YOU CAN MAKE YOUR CHARACTER ANY SHAPE YOU WANT... USING THE SAME BASIC CONSTRUCTION.

THIS CHARACTER
HAS AN OVAL AND
A CIRCLE FOR A HEAD.

THE BODY IS
EGG-SHAPED.

STOVEPIPE LEGS

COMPLETE THIS FIGURE USING YOUR OWN IDEAS
FOR THE FINISHING DETAILS.

FINISH THESE CHARACTERS:

ACTION LINE

THE ACTION LINE IS EXACTLY AS IT SOUNDS - A LINE THAT RUNS THROUGH THE CENTER OF YOUR CHARACTER WHICH DETERMINES ITS DIRECTION OR COURSE OF ACTION. OF COURSE, THIS IS AN IMAGINARY LINE!

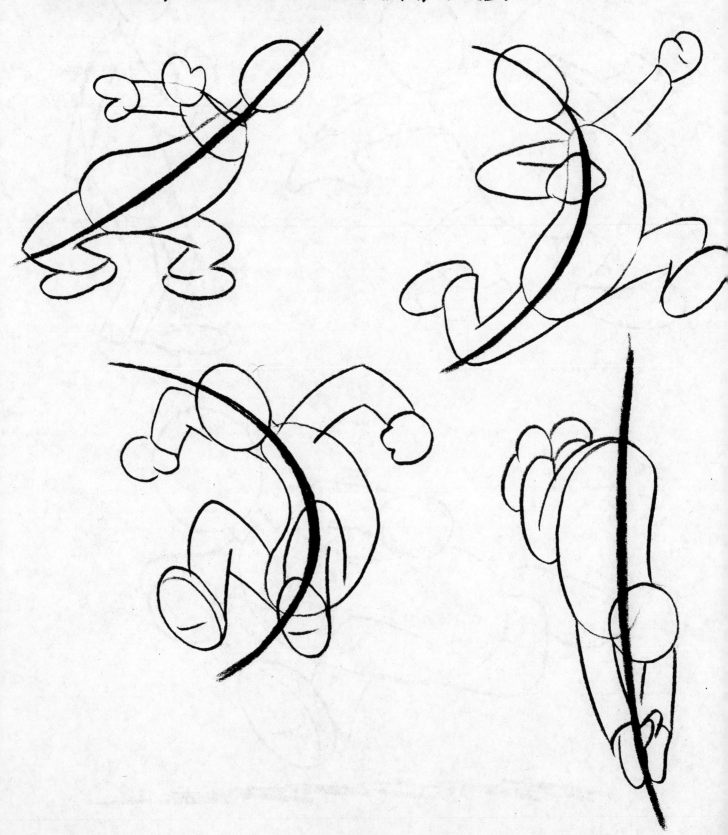

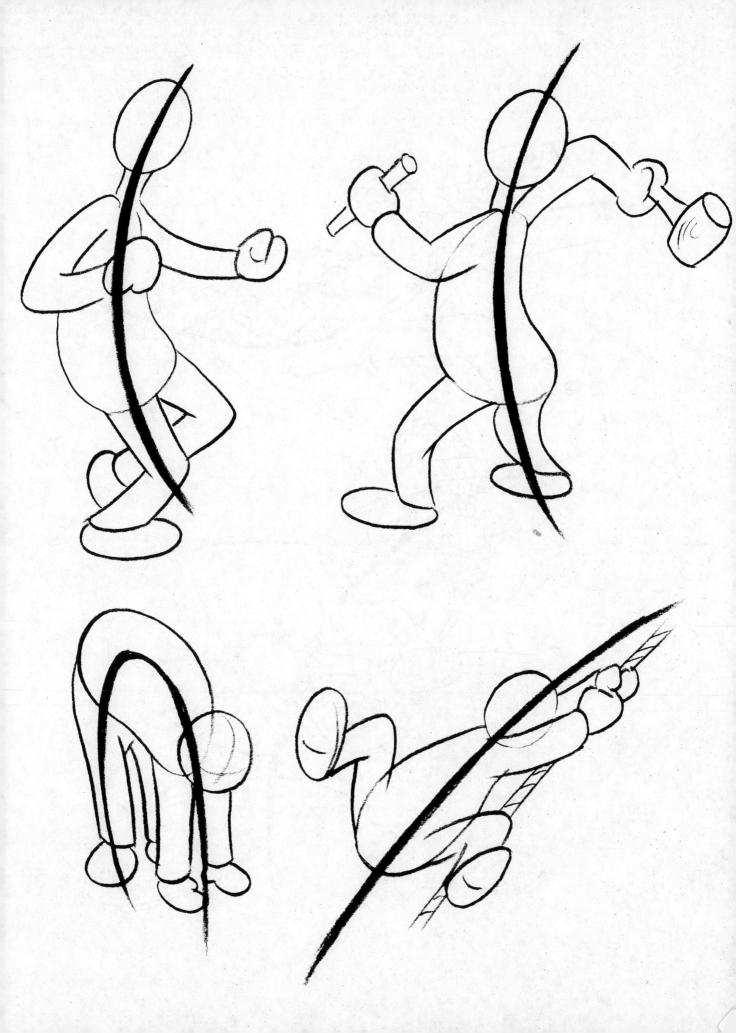

THE ACTION LINE IS PRESENT IN FOUR-LEGGED CHARACTERS, AS WELL AS IN THE TWO-LEGGED TYPE.

THE SAME BASIC RULES OF CONSTRUCTION APPLY TO THE
FOUR-LEGGED CHARACTER.

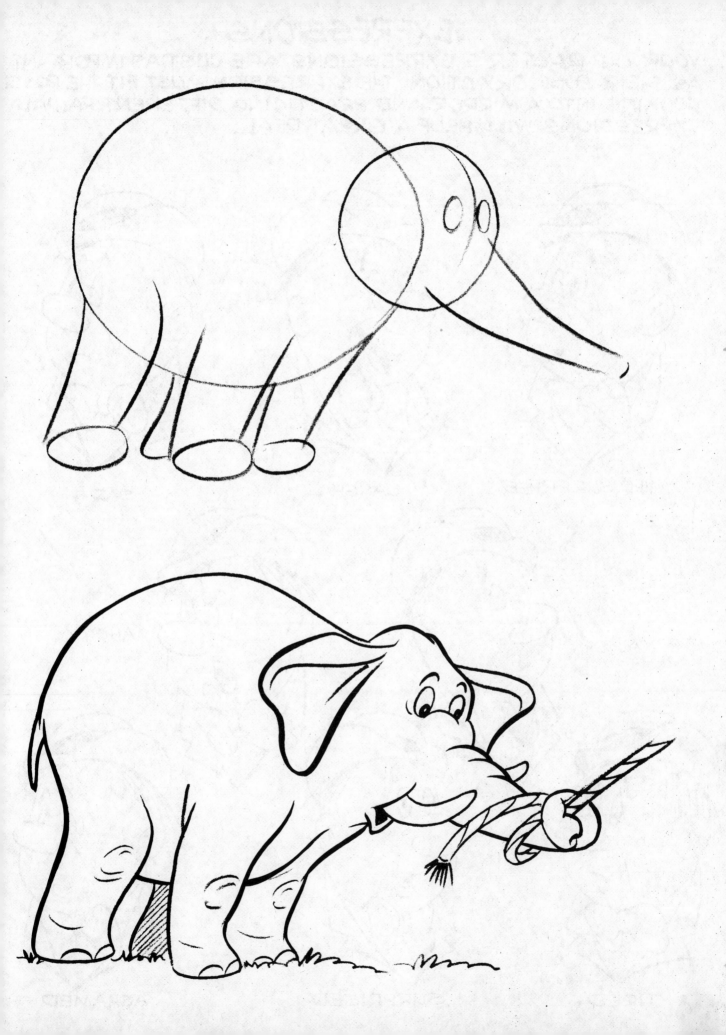

EXPRESSIONS
YOUR CHARACTER'S EXPRESSIONS ARE JUST AS IMPORTANT
AS THEIR POSE OR ACTION. THE EXPRESSION MUST FIT THE POSE.
LOOKING INTO A MIRROR AND PRACTICING DIFFERENT FACIAL
EXPRESSIONS WILL HELP A GREAT DEAL.

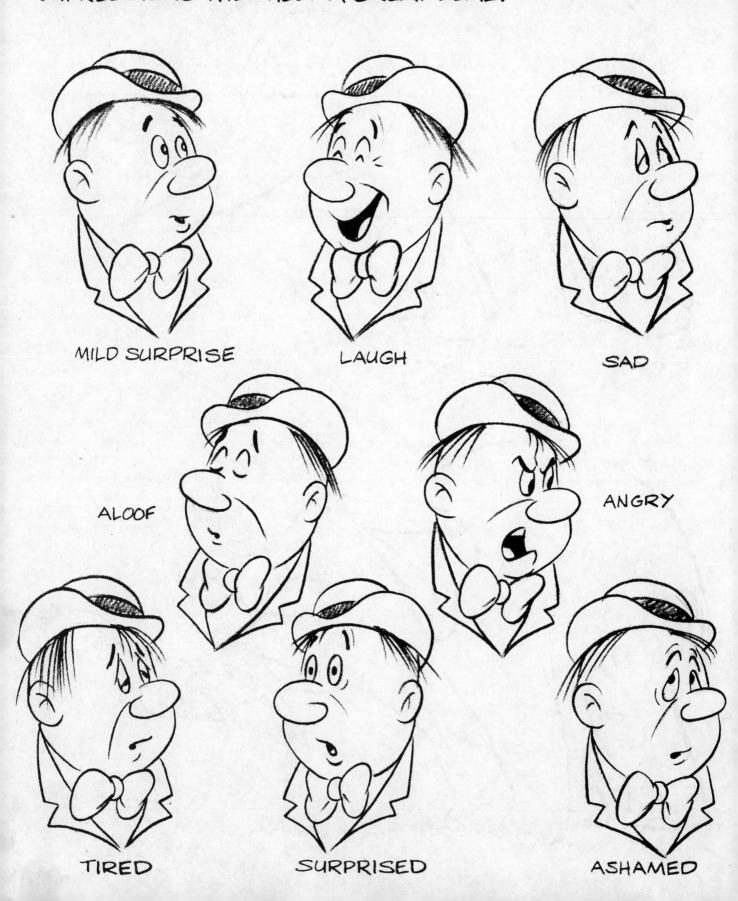

MILD SURPRISE

LAUGH

SAD

ALOOF

ANGRY

TIRED

SURPRISED

ASHAMED

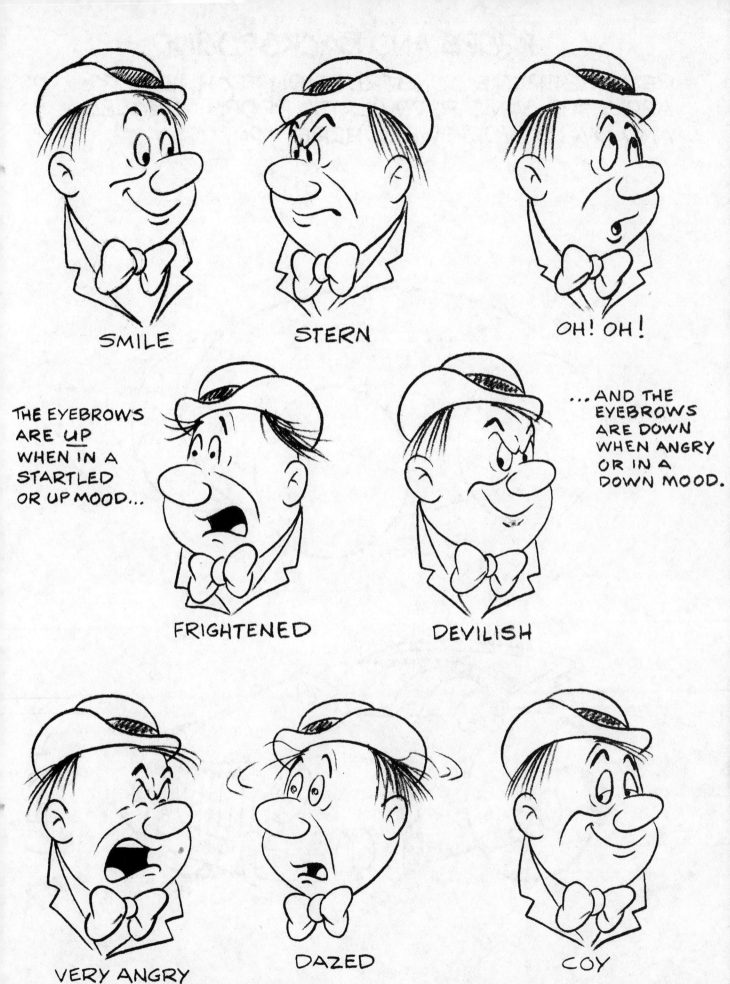

SMILE

STERN

OH! OH!

THE EYEBROWS
ARE UP
WHEN IN A
STARTLED
OR UP MOOD...

FRIGHTENED

DEVILISH

...AND THE
EYEBROWS
ARE DOWN
WHEN ANGRY
OR IN A
DOWN MOOD.

VERY ANGRY

DAZED

COY

PROPS AND BACKGROUND

REMEMBER THE CONSTRUCTION TECHNIQUE?
APPLY THE SAME FORMULA TO PROPS. CIRCLES
AND OVALS WORK WELL HERE, TOO.

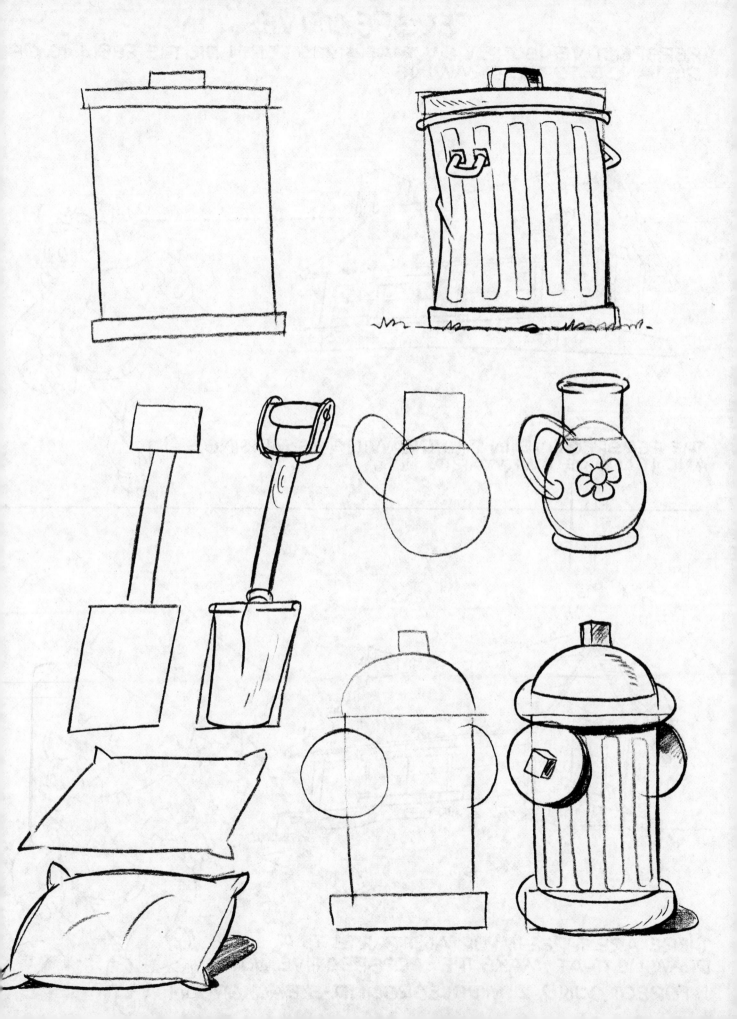

PERSPECTIVE

PERSPECTIVE IS THE VIEW THAT GIVES DEPTH OR THE FEELING OF DISTANCE TO THE DRAWING.

THE PERSPECTIVE IN THIS DRAWING IS MISSING, AND IT LOOKS AWKWARD.

THERE ARE THREE IMPORTANT PARTS TO A DRAWING THAT MAKE THE PERSPECTIVE WORK:
1. FOREGROUND 2. MIDDLEGROUND 3. BACKGROUND

SHADING
SHADING GIVES YOUR DRAWING A FINISHED LOOK.
WITHOUT SHADOWS, THIS DRAWING IS INCOMPLETE.

DECIDE WHERE YOUR LIGHT SOURCE IS COMING FROM.
THE OPPOSITE SIDE OF YOUR CHARACTERS OR OBJECTS
WILL CAST A SHADOW. STUDY THE SHADING BELOW.

A HAT MAY START OUT
LOOKING LIKE THIS...

...BUT IT SHOULD END UP WITH
DIMENSION, TO FIT ON THE HEAD.

THE SAME IS TRUE WITH ANY OBJECT THAT IS ROUND OR OVAL.

TREES ARE USED IN CARTOON BACKGROUNDS MORE THAN ANY OTHER OBJECT.

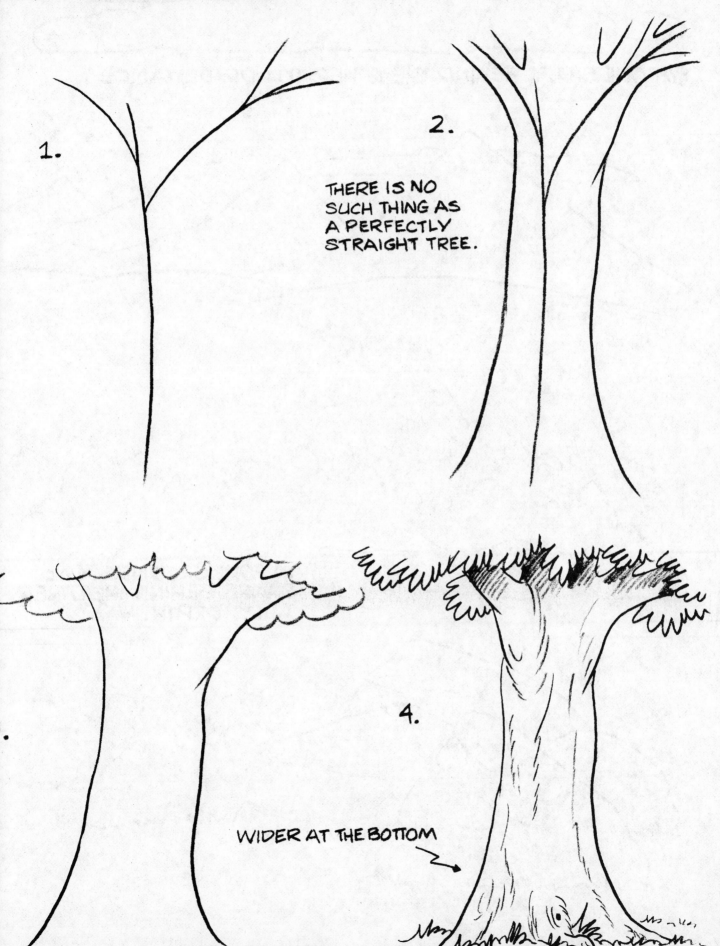

1.

2.

THERE IS NO SUCH THING AS A PERFECTLY STRAIGHT TREE.

3.

4.

WIDER AT THE BOTTOM

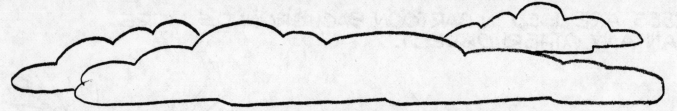

PUT ONE SHAPE BEHIND THE OTHER TO ADD DISTANCE.

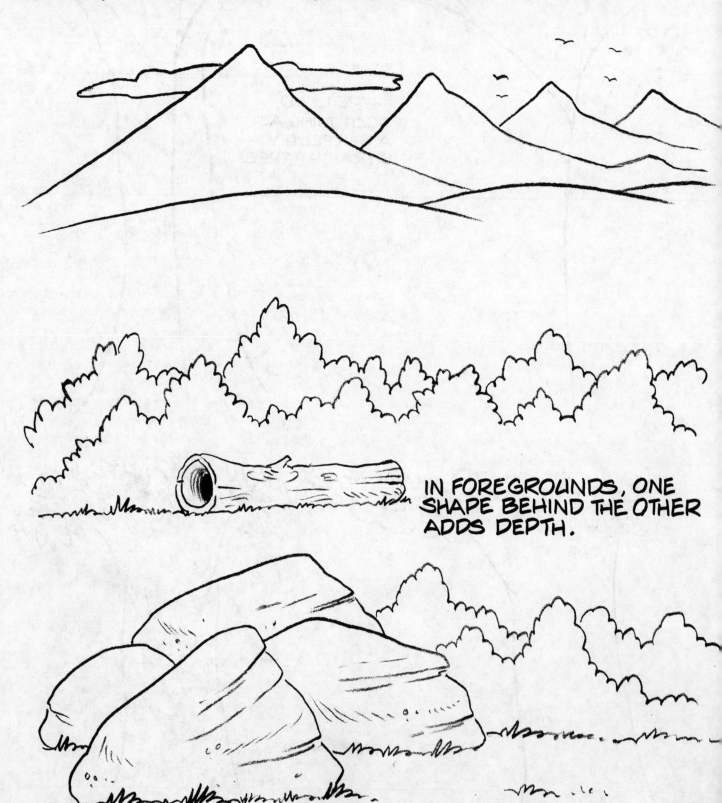

IN FOREGROUNDS, ONE
SHAPE BEHIND THE OTHER
ADDS DEPTH.

BACKGROUND

MIDDLEGROUND

FOREGROUND

1.

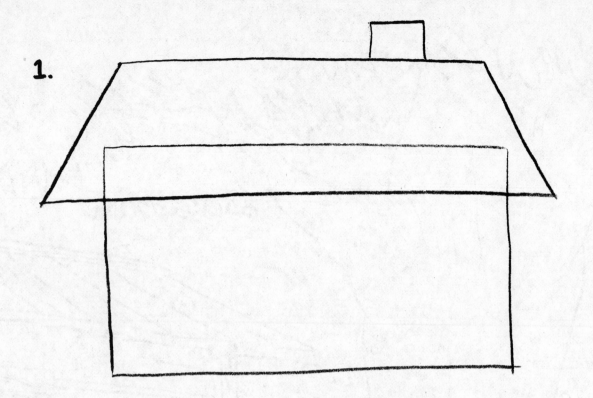

HOUSES ARE EASY TO DRAW.

2.

REMEMBER,
A HOUSE
HAS MORE
THAN ONE
SIDE.

GIVE IT DEP

FINISH THIS COUNTRY SCENE:

STUDY THE DRAWINGS ON THE OPPOSITE PAGE, THEN
COMPLETE THE ROUGH SKETCH BELOW.

DRAWING CARTOON CHILDREN

CHILDREN IN CARTOONS ARE NOT SIMPLY SMALL ADULTS.

NOTE THE SIZE OF THE HEAD AND BODY. THEY ARE BASICALLY THE SAME.

IF YOU DIVIDE THE CIRCLE IN HALF, THE EYES, NOSE, AND MOUTH ARE ALL IN THE LOWER HALF.

THE LARGE FOREHEAD GIVES THE CHARACTER A MUCH YOUNGER LOOK.

THIS IS ONE STYLE OF DRAWING CHILDREN. HOWEVER, THE BASIC RULES APPLY IN ALMOST ANY CARTOON STYLE.

KEEP YOUR LINES
SOFT-LOOKING.

DRAWING YOUR OWN COMIC STRIP

THE FIRST STEP IS TO DECIDE ON WHAT <u>SIZE</u> YOU WANT TO DRAW YOUR COMIC STRIP.

1.

CUT OUT YOUR FAVORITE COMIC STRIP FROM THE DAILY NEWSPAPER.

2.

TAPE IT TO A LARGE SHEET OF PAPER. BE SURE IT IS POSITIONE AT THE LEFT-HAND SIDE OF THE PAPER.

3.

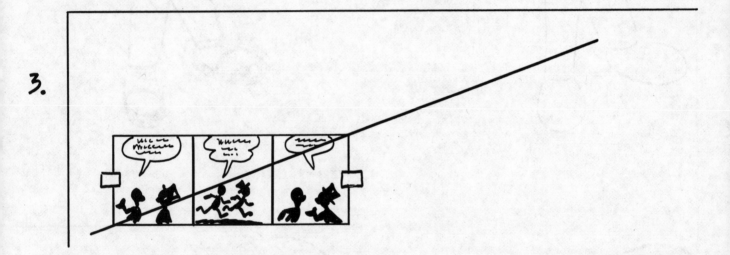

WITH A RULER OR STRAIGHT EDGE, DRAW A LINE FROM THE LOWER LEFT-HAND CORNER OF THE COMIC STRIP THROUGH THE UPPER RIGHT-HAND CORNER.

4.

CONTINUE THE LEFT BORDER LINE OF THE COMIC STRIP.

CONTINUE THE BOTTOM BORDER LINE.

5.

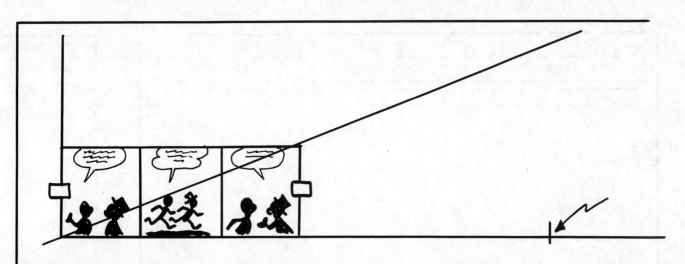

ALONG THE BOTTOM LINE, PICK A SPOT THAT YOU THINK WOULD BE LARGE ENOUGH FOR YOU TO WORK IN.

6.

DRAW A LINE STRAIGHT UP FROM THAT POINT.

7.

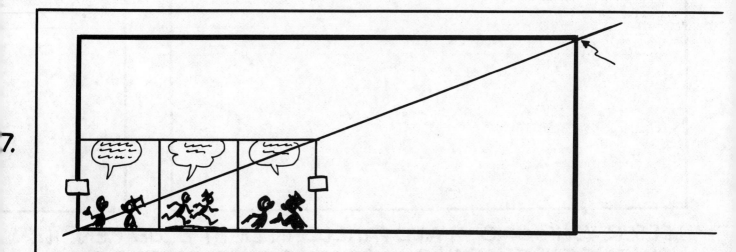

AT THE POINT WHERE THE TWO LINES ON THE RIGHT SIDE MEET, DRAW A LINE STRAIGHT ACROSS THE TOP. THIS IS NOW THE SIZE OF YOUR COMIC STRIP. ALWAYS WORK IN THIS SAME SIZE.

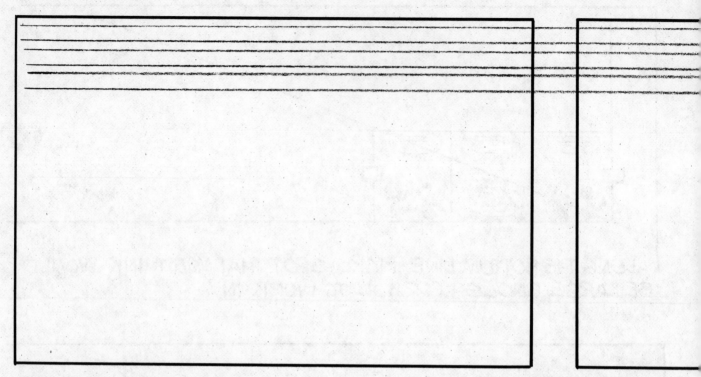

FIRST RULE THE PANELS IN INK. NEXT, RULE LETTERING LINES IN LIGHT BLUE PENCIL.

LETTER YOUR GAG IN ALL PANELS IN LIGHT BLUE PENCIL. NOW PUT THE SPEECH BALLOONS AROUND YOUR LETTERING.

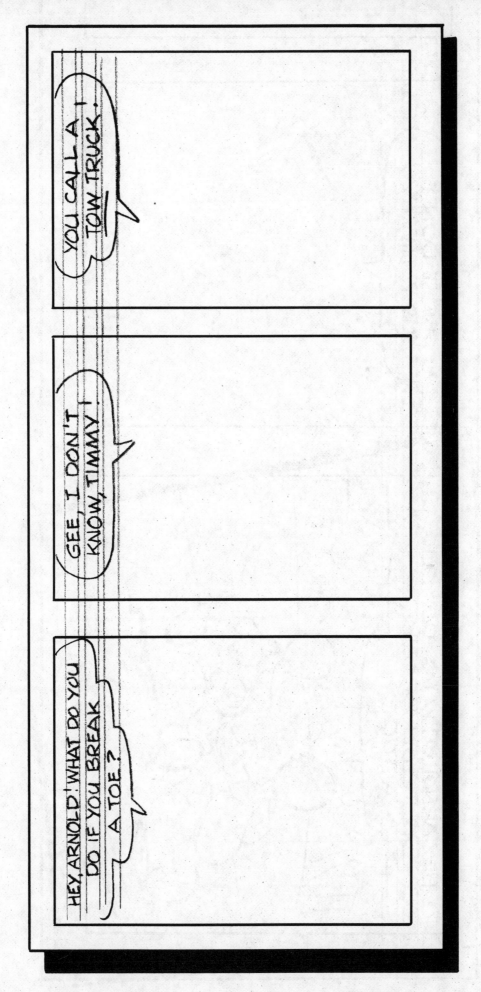

WITH THE LETTERING PENCILED IN POSITION, YOU NOW KNOW HOW MUCH ROOM
YOU HAVE TO DRAW THE CHARACTERS IN THE COMIC STRIP.

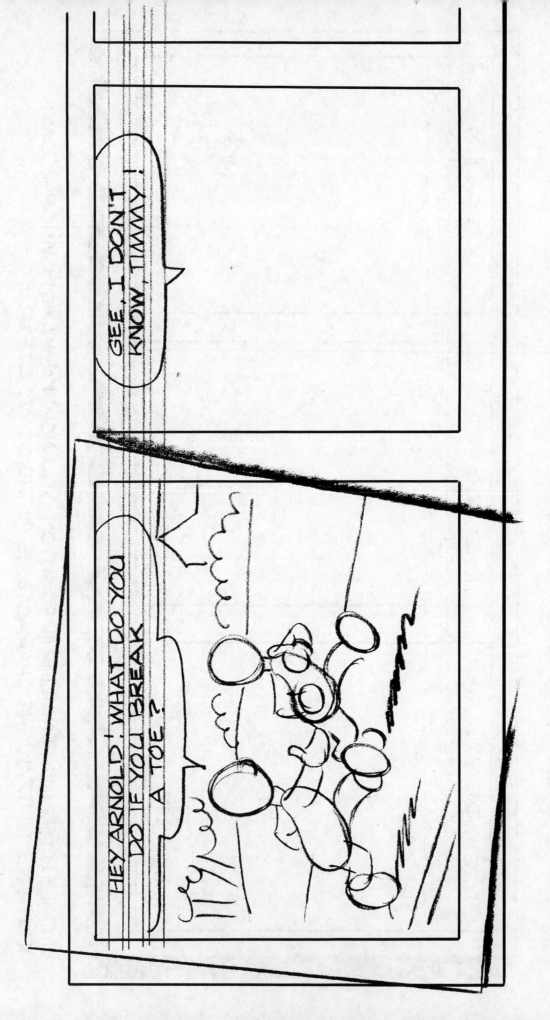

LAY A PIECE OF TRACING PAPER OVER THE FIRST PANEL, AND START TO ROUGH-IN YOUR CHARACTERS IN BLUE PENCIL.

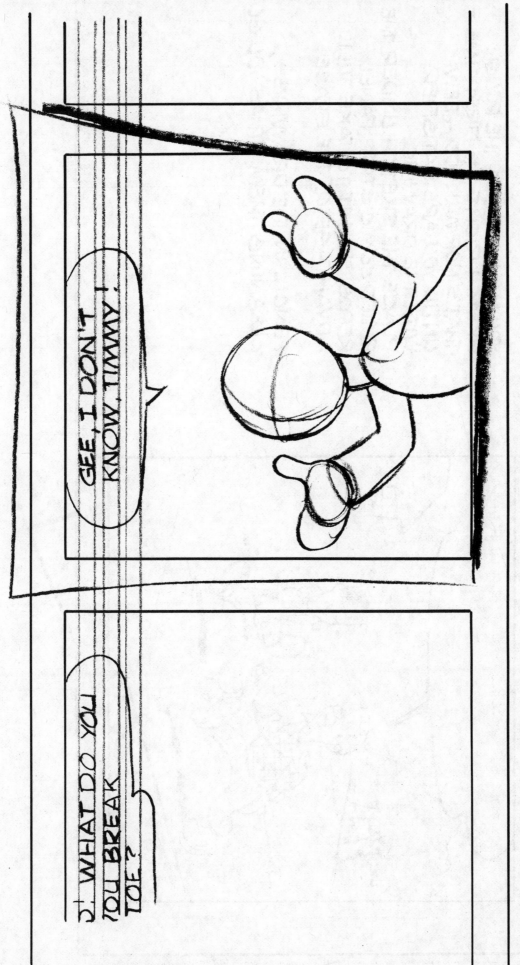

ROUGH SKETCH THE ENTIRE STRIP AS YOU DID IN THE FIRST PANEL.

YOU MAY NOT GET THE ROUGH
SKETCH RIGHT THE FIRST TIME -
THAT'S NORMAL. DO A FEW
UNTIL YOU ARE SATISFIED
WITH THE DRAWING.
PLACE THE SKETCH UNDER THE
RULED COMIC STRIP PANEL.
REPOSITION IT TO TAKE FULL
ADVANTAGE OF THE SPACE.

PENCIL-IN THE DRAWINGS,
CLEANING THEM UP AS YOU GO.

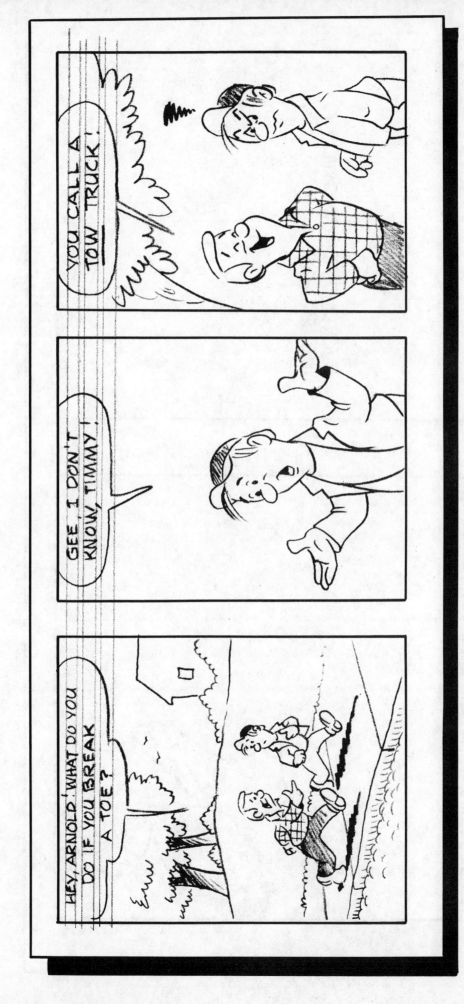

ALL YOU NEED TO DO NOW IS INK THE STRIP AND IT'S FINISHED!

AVOID OVERCROWDING
THE PANEL...

OR TOO MUCH
WHITE SPACE...

OR

CHOPPING OFF THE
CHARACTER'S HEAD...

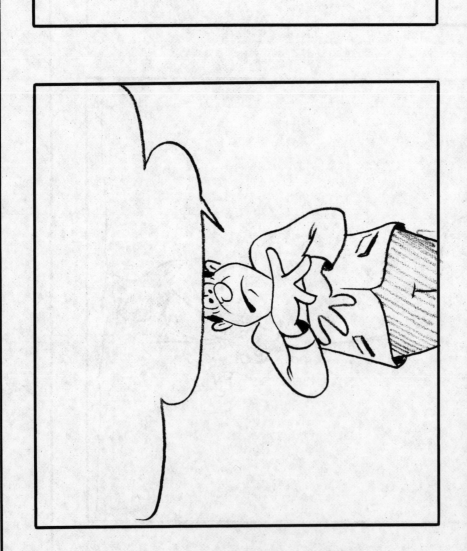

OR
CHOPPING OFF THE
CHARACTER'S FEET!

IF YOU NEED TO CROP OR CUT OFF PART OF A CHARACTER, BE SURE TO LEAVE ENOUGH TO TELL THE STORY.

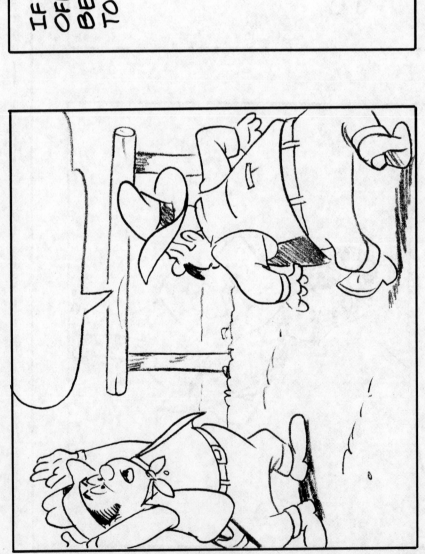

WHEN LAYING OUT YOUR COMIC STRIP, IT IS ALWAYS BEST TO ESTABLISH THE SCENE OR SETTING FIRST.

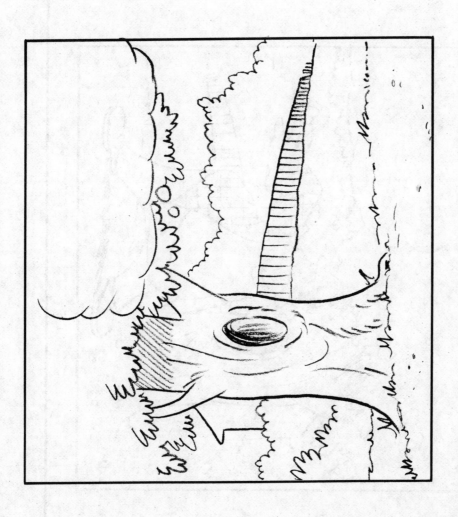

PLACE YOUR CHARACTER
SO THAT IT FITS INTO
THE SCENE.

YOUR COMIC STRIP SHOULD
BE INTERESTING TO LOOK AT.
PROPER STAGING CAN HELP
ACCOMPLISH THIS.

THE CLOSEUP!

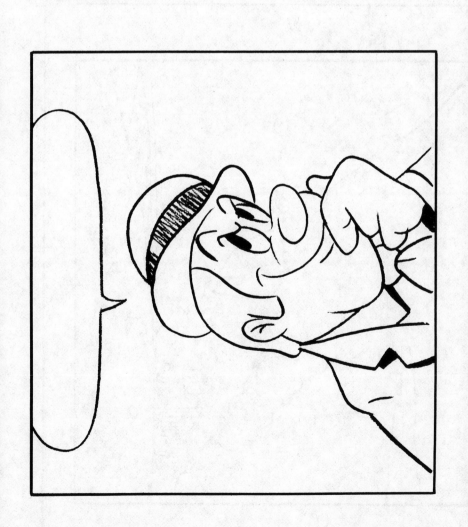

THE LONG SHOT

THE SILHOUETTE

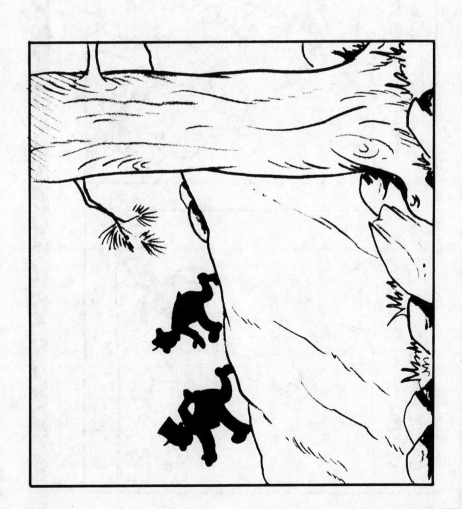

WRITING GAGS FOR A COMIC STRIP IS SIMPLY TELLING A JOKE WITH PICTURES!

THE FIRST PANEL
SETS UP THE GAG!

THE MIDDLE PANEL (OR
PANELS) EXPLAINS IT...

...AND THE LAST PANEL
DELIVERS THE PUNCH LINE!

THE FINISHED STRIP

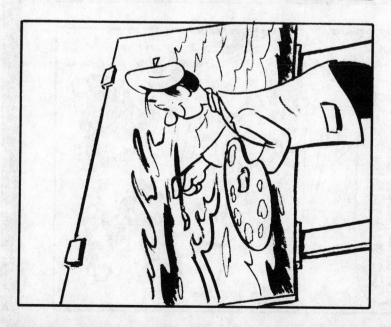

IT LOOKS EASY, DOESN'T IT? IT IS EASY, IF YOU PRACTICE! REMEMBER, THE MOST IMPORTANT RULE OF ALL IN CARTOONING IS, "HAVE FUN DOING IT!"